Young Learner'

LOOK-n-LEARN
OUR UNIVERSE

Sky

The sky is everything located above the surface of the Earth. The sky on Earth appears blue as our atmosphere scatters the blue colour from the sunlight.

Universe

The universe is a large expanse of dust, gas, stars, clouds and clusters of galaxies together. Objects in the universe are always radiating energy.

Big Bang

Big Bang refers to the rapid expansion of matter due to cosmic explosion. Scientists believe that the universe originated this way.

Galaxy

A galaxy is a system of billions of stars together with gas and dust. They are held together by gravitational force. Most galaxies are found in clusters.

Milky Way

Our Solar System is a part of the Milky Way galaxy. There are more than 100 billion stars in Milky Way. It is a spiral galaxy and has a bulge in the centre.

Star

A star is a giant spinning ball of hot gases. It gives out huge amounts of heat and light. Betelgeuse star is about 800 times the size of the Sun.

Sun

The Sun is a star at the centre of our Solar System. We get heat and light from it. It is mainly made of hydrogen and helium.

Constellation

A constellation is a group of stars that form a pattern. There are 88 constellations. The largest constellation, Hydra, contains about 68 stars.

Heliosphere

The heliosphere is the vast region around the Sun. It extends from the Sun to about 15 billion miles well beyond the orbit of Pluto.

Sunspots

Sunspots are dark patches found on the surface of the Sun. They appear to be dark as they are cooler than the rest of the Sun's surface.

Solar flare

Solar flare is a storm on the Sun. It appears as a very bright red spot. It is extremely hot and releases huge amounts of gases and particles.

Solar eclipse

During the solar eclipse, the Moon comes directly between the Earth and the Sun. The Moon casts its shadow on the Earth.

Satellite

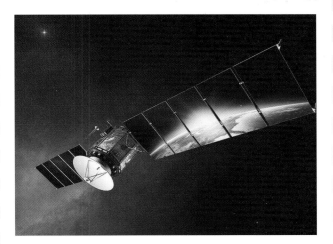

A satellite is an object that orbits a planet. There are several natural and artificial satellites in the Solar System. Sputnik 1 was the first artificial satellite.

Moon

A moon is the natural satellite of a planet. It is a rocky world that orbits a planet. Our Earth has one moon. Venus has no moon.

Ray craters

Ray craters are circular depressions on Moon, formed due to volcanic activity or meteorite strikes. The rays extend to hundreds of kilometres.

Olympus Mons

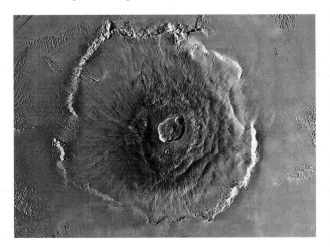

Olympus Mons is a volcano on Mars. Situated on the edge of the Tharsis Ridge, it is the tallest mountain in the Solar System. It is about 27 km high.

Solar System

The Sun, eight major planets, three dwarf planets, their moons, asteroids, meteoroids, comets, gases and dust together form the Solar System.

Planet

A planet is a large body that moves around the Sun. There are 8 major planets and 3 dwarf planets in our Solar System.

Mercury

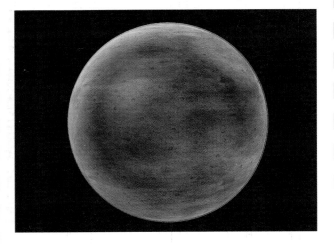

Mercury is the planet closest to the Sun. It can be seen from the Earth late in the evening or early in the morning. Its skies always remain black.

Venus

Venus is Earth's sister planet. It has many mountains and volcanoes on its surface. Its atmosphere is made of unbreathable carbon dioxide.

Earth

Earth is the only known planet to have liquid flowing water on its surface. It is also the only known planet that can support life.

Mars

Mars is also known as the Red Planet as the surface of the planet is red. It has many extinct volcanoes. Mars has two moons called Phobos and Deimos.

Jupiter

Jupiter is the biggest planet in the Solar System. It is big enough to contain all the other planets put together. It is known as a Gas Giant. It has 63 known moons.

Saturn

Saturn is the second largest planet. It is the least dense of the planets. It has three main rings and many less-dense rings made up of ice, dust and rocks.

Uranus

Uranus is a gigantic ball of gas. The atmosphere of the planet contains methane, hydrogen and helium. It is often referred to as Ice Giant.

Neptune

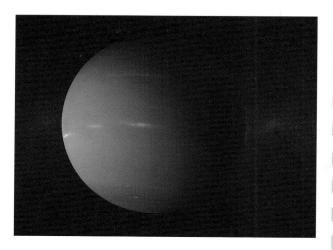

Neptune is farthest from the Sun. It is the coldest and windiest planet in the Solar System. It has 14 known moons. It is the smallest of the ice giants.

Pluto

Pluto is a dwarf planet. It lies in the Kuiper belt. It has 5 known moons. The largest moon is called Charon. Pluto is named after the Greek god of underworld.

Ceres

Ceres is a dwarf planet in the asteroid belt lying between Mars and Jupiter. It is the largest and most massive body in the asteroid belt. It has no moons.

Great Red Spot

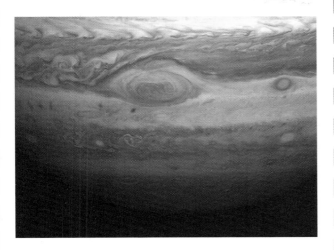

The Great Red Spot is a cloud belt on Jupiter. The multicoloured gases in Jupiter's atmosphere, whirling at high speeds, create many cloud belts.

Supernova

A supernova is a huge explosion caused when a supergiant star explodes. The star ends up as a neutron star or black hole.

Crab nebula

Crab nebula is the remains of a supernova. It consists of dust and gas slowly drifting off into space. It was first identified in 1731.

Red dwarf

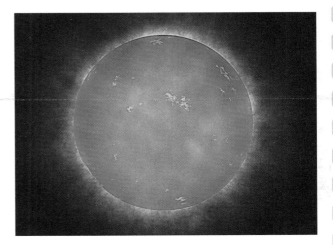

Red dwarf is a small, faint and cool star. Its surface temperature is under 4,000 K. Proxima Centauri is a red dwarf, discovered in 1915.

White dwarf

A white dwarf is a small star near the end of its life. It is so dense that one teaspoonful of its matter would weigh as much as an elephant on Earth.

Blue giant

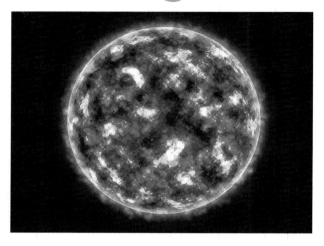

Blue giant stars are large and very hot blue stars. They burn helium. They have at least 18 times the mass of the Sun.

Kuiper belt

The Kuiper belt is a ring that extends beyond the orbit of Neptune. It contains thousands of small and slow-moving icy bodies.

Quasar

Quasars are distant objects in space. Some of them give out huge amounts of radiation. They were first detected in 1963–64.

Asteroid

Asteroids are small, irregular-shaped objects that orbit the Sun between Mars and Jupiter. Most asteroids are rocky but some are also made of metal.

Quaoar

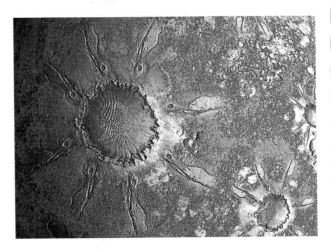

Quaoar is a large object that lies in the Kuiper belt. It was discovered in 2002. It is made of ice and rock. It is over half the diameter of Pluto.

Meteorite

Sometimes, small fragments of rocks from space hit the Earth's surface. These are called meteorites. They range in size from tiny fragments to huge boulders.

Meteor shower

A meteor shower occurs when many meteoroids enter the atmosphere, lighting up the sky. They appear to radiate from one point in the sky.

Comet

A comet is a small object made up of dust and ice. It appears like a small white ball with a tail. It orbits the Sun.

Halley's Comet

Halley's Comet is a comet that is visible from Earth every 75–76 years. It last appeared in 1986. It will be next seen in 2061.

Shooting star

A shooting star is not a star, but a small fragment that has broken off from a comet. It is a streak of light that lasts usually for less than a second.

Oort Cloud

Oort Cloud is made of billions of icy objects. It surrounds the Solar System. It may be the birthplace of long-period comets.

Scattered Disc

Scattered Disc is a region which lies just beyond the Kuiper Belt. Dwarf planet Eris lies in this disc and is the largest known object in the disc.

Virgo Cluster

The Virgo Cluster is a huge cluster of galaxies. There are approximately 2000 galaxies, including dwarf galaxies, in this cluster.

Black hole

A black hole is the remains of a star. Its gravity is so strong that nothing, not even light, can escape from it. It has a mass roughly 10 times that of Sun.

Nebula

A nebula is a cloud of dust and gases such as hydrogen, helium, etc. New stars are formed when nebula compresses under force of gravity.

Dark matter

Scientists say that there is dark matter in space, which influences things such as the rotation, size and shape of galaxies.

Astronomy

Astronomy is the study of heavenly bodies such as stars, asteroids, comets, etc. It is one of the oldest science studies.

Astronomer

Astronomers are people who study heavenly bodies. They are professionals who work in observatories and study the universe.

Astronaut

An astronaut is trained to command or work as a crew member in a spacecraft. The first woman astronaut was Valentina Tereshkova.

Spacecraft

A spacecraft is a vehicle used to travel to space. It has its own engines and rocket boosters. It may or may not carry people.

NASA

NASA or the National Aeronautics and Space Administration in the USA is an agency that is responsible for space programmes of the US.

International Space Station

The International Space Station (ISS) is the biggest object sent to space. It is a joint venture between USA, Russia, Canada and other countries.

Sputnik 1

Sputnik 1 was the first artificial satellite launched in 1957. It orbited the Earth in a low elliptical orbit. It was visible from all around the Earth.

Soyuz

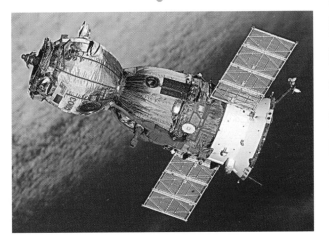

Soyuz is a Russian spacecraft in use since 1967. It can carry three people and supplies to and from the space station. It was launched in April 1967.

Ulysses

Ulysses was a space probe that was launched in 1990. It orbited the Sun to study its magnetism, poles and latitudes. It is no longer in use.

SOHO

SOHO is the Solar and Heliospheric Observatory, designed to study the Sun and take its images. It was launched on December 2, 1995.

Rosetta

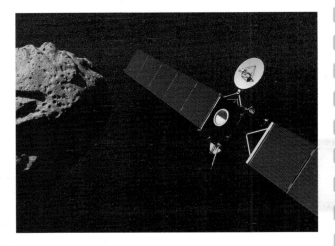

Rosetta is the spacecraft sent into space by European Space Agency to obtain details of asteroids and comets. It was launched in 2004.